Catholic Update
guide to
Faithful
Citizenship

MARY CAROL KENDZIA
Series Editor

ST. ANTHONY MESSENGER PRESS
Cincinnati, Ohio

RESCRIPT

In accord with the *Code of Canon Law,* I hereby grant the Imprimatur
("Permission to Publish") to
Catholic Update Guide to Faithful Citizenship

Most Reverend Joseph R. Binzer
Vicar General and Auxiliary Bishop
Archdiocese of Cincinnati
Cincinnati, Ohio
February 8, 2012

Cover and book design by Mark Sullivan.
Cover image © klikk | photoxpress

LIBRARY OF CONGRESS CATALOGING-IN-PUBLICATION DATA

Catholic update guide to faithful citizenship / Mary Carol Kendzia, series editor.
p. cm.
Includes bibliographical references (p.   ).
ISBN 978-1-61636-411-3 (alk. paper)
1. Lord's Supper—Catholic Church. 2. Catholic Church—Doctrines. I. Kendzia,
Mary Carol.
BX2215.3.C44 2012
234'.163—dc23

2011042890

ISBN 978-1-61636-411-3

Published by St. Anthony Messenger Press
28 W. Liberty St.
Cincinnati, OH 45202
www.AmericanCatholic.org
www.SAMPBooks.org

Printed in the United States of America.
Printed on acid-free paper.
12 13 14 15 16   5 4 3 2 1

Contents

About This Series

The Catholic Update guides take the best material from our best-selling newsletters and videos to bring you up-to-the-minute resources for your faith. Topically arranged for these books, the words you'll find in these pages are the same clear, concise, authoritative information you've come to expect from the nation's most trusted faith formation series. Plus, we've designed this series with a practical focus—giving the "what," "why," and "how to" for the people in the pews.

The series takes the topics most relevant to parish life—for example, the Mass, sacraments, Scripture, the liturgical year—and draws them out in a fresh and straightforward way. The books can be read by individuals or used in a study group. They are an invaluable resource for sacramental preparation, RCIA participants, faith formation, and liturgical ministry training, and are a great tool for everyday Catholics who want to brush up on the basics.

The content for the series comes from noted authors such as Thomas Richstatter, O.F.M., Lawrence Mick, Leonard Foley, O.F.M., Carol Luebering, William H. Shannon, and others. Their theology and approach is grounded in Catholic practice and tradition, while mindful of current Church practice and teaching. We blend each author's style and approach into a voice that is clear, unified, and eminently readable.

Enrich your knowledge and practice of the Catholic faith with the helpful topics in the Catholic Update Guide series.

Mary Carol Kendzia
Series Editor

Introduction

The *Catholic Update Guide to Faithful Citizenship* provides, in *Catholic Update*'s well-known, substantial-yet-popular style, a look at moral issues that are relevant to making an informed decision in the voting booth, one that is grounded in the teachings of the Catholic faith. The book is inspired by the U.S. Catholic bishops' document, *Forming Consciences for Faithful Citizenship: A Call to Political Responsibility*, a pre-election reflection on these same issues—the political, moral, and social questions that have a bearing on our lives, which of necessity must be addressed by the presidential candidates.

This book does not tell people how to vote; rather, the hope is that it will help people to understand their faith more deeply. For example, it echoes the bishops' observation that we are: "an affluent society where too many live in poverty; part of a global community confronting and facing urgent threats to the environment; a culture built on families where some now question the value of marriage and family life. We pride ourselves on supporting human rights, but we fail even to protect the fundamental right to life, especially for unborn children."

The list of authors and contributors to this book includes many Church leaders of high moral authority, such as Pope John XXIII, Pope John Paul II, Archbishop Wilton Gregory, and Daniel Pilarczyk, as well as moral theologians such as Richard Gula, S.S., Kenneth Overberg, S.J., and ethicist Thomas Shannon. These and many other experts explain key moral, social, and political principles that will help voters in the United States make wise choices when they go to the polls.

The book reflects the best of our *Catholic Updates* covering the themes our bishops ask us to reflect on before elections. It focuses not only on the forming of human conscience, but also on applying that conscience to the way we vote. Whether the themes are human life issues or our responsibility to the world, our Catholic faith has something to say.

—Jack Wintz, O.F.M., founding editor, *Catholic Update*

CHAPTER ONE

The Challenge of Forming Consciences

Before every national election in the United States, our Catholic bishops issue a call to "faithful citizenship." Are they telling people how to vote? Not at all! Faithful citizenship refers to the responsibility of each of us to have an informed conscience, and to use that informed conscience in making all of our decisions, including voting decisions. Church leadership has an obligation to help us form our consciences and, by doing so, helps us become faithful citizens.

The Church speaks clearly on the issues themselves. We turn to the Church to learn what our faith teaches about critical issues of our time, such as matters of war and peace, poverty, and safeguarding life from conception to natural death. In all these issues, our faith, in both Scripture and tradition, informs our decision-making.

American and Catholic

The introductory note to the 2011 statement urges Catholics "to contribute to civil and respectful public dialogue, and to shape their choices in the coming election in the light of Catholic teaching."

We have a "dual heritage," say the bishops, both as Catholics and as American citizens. We have a duty to participate in public life. "Our Church, through its institutions, must be free to carry out its mission and contribute to the common good without being pressured to sacrifice fundamental teachings and moral principles."

The principle of the common good is a cherished American institution that ought to drive Catholics to participate in the political process. What do we mean by "common good"? It's the conditions—spiritual, social and material—that are needed in a society in order for each person to recognize and realize his or her full human dignity.

The bishops note, by the way, that it isn't solely an American initiative to bring Catholic teaching to bear on social issues. Within the long tradition of popes and bishops who cried out for justice, they quote the Second Vatican Council document

Declaration on Religious Liberty (*Dignitatis Humanae*) which says that "society itself may enjoy the benefits of justice and peace, which result from [people's] faithfulness to God and his holy will" (6). The bishops add, "The work for justice requires that the mind and the heart of Catholics be educated and formed to know and practice the whole faith."

In the end, the bishops advocate for an approach to politics in our country that is not polarized or ideological. They plea for a "new kind of politics: Focused more on moral principles than on the latest polls; focused more on the needs of the weak than on benefits for the strong; focused more on the pursuit of the common good than on the demands of narrow interest."

That, they say, will honor both our Catholic tradition and "the best traditions of our nation."

Some Guidelines for Parishes

Parishioners often complain that their parishes are stepping into politics inappropriately, or, conversely, not taking positions for candidates who are "obviously more in line with Catholicism." The USCCB offers a few pointers for parish leaders:

Do

- Share the seven principles of Catholic social teaching
- Encourage voter participation in a nonpartisan way
- Support or oppose political issues that will be ballot measures (such as social issues and tax levies)
- Promote or provide nonpartisan voter education

Don't
- Endorse or oppose candidates or political parties
- Use any Church facilities or assets for partisan political purposes
- Distribute any partisan political materials (materials that support or oppose any political candidate or party)
- Invite only select candidates to address parish gatherings

When Church leaders make judgments about how to apply Catholic teaching to specific policies, this may not carry the same binding authority as universal moral principles but cannot be dismissed as one political opinion among others. These moral applications should inform the consciences and guide the actions of Catholics.

The bishops refer to seven key themes in Catholic social teaching to help Catholic voters in assessing candidates' positions and their potential impact upon public life:

1. The right to life and the dignity of the human person. Human life is sacred. Direct attacks on innocent human beings are never morally acceptable. In addition, life is under direct attack from abortion, euthanasia, human cloning, and destruction of human embryos for research. These intrinsic evils must always be opposed.

2. Call to family, community, and participation. The family, based on marriage between a man and a woman, is the fundamental unit of society. Supporting families should be a priority for economic and social policies.

3. Rights and responsibilities. Each of us has a right to life, a right to religious freedom, a right to access to those things required for human decency—food and shelter, education and employment, health care and housing.

4. Option for the poor and vulnerable. While the common good embraces all, those who are in greatest need deserve preferential concern. A moral test for society is how we treat the weakest among us—the unborn, those dealing with disabilities or terminal illness, the poor and marginalized.

5. Dignity of work and the rights of workers. The economy must serve people, not the other way around. Economic justice calls for decent work at fair, living wages, opportunities for legal status for immigrant workers, and the opportunity for all people to work together for the common good through their work, ownership, enterprise, investment, participation in unions, and other forms of economic activity.

6. Solidarity. We are one human family, whatever our national, racial, ethnic, economic, and ideological differences. Our Catholic commitment to solidarity requires that we pursue justice, eliminate racism, end human trafficking, protect human rights, seek peace, and avoid the use of force except as a necessary last resort.

7. Caring for God's creation. Care for the earth is a duty of our Catholic faith. We all are called to be careful stewards of God's creation and to ensure a safe and hospitable environment for vulnerable human beings now and in the future.

* * *

One of the more ticklish and controversial elements in the bishops' document is their conclusion that although a Catholic should not vote for a candidate favoring an intrinsic evil such as abortion or racism, there may be circumstances in which a voter who rejects a candidate's unacceptable position on a given issue may vote for that candidate for other morally grave reasons. This admission is finely tuned and requires delicate analysis. Voters must be morally discerning, recognizing that not all issues carry the same moral gravity, but at the same time opposition to intrinsically evil acts has a special claim on our consciences and actions.

Questions for Reflection

1. Does *Forming Consciences for Faithful Citizenship* violation the idea of the separation of Church and state?
2. Which political issues might be termed "intrinsically evil"?
3. Of the seven themes listed by the U.S. bishops' statement, which do you think is most supported by Americans? The most ignored?

CHAPTER TWO

Conscience and Voting

We know our conscience must guide us when difficult decisions are to be made. We speak of doing things in "good conscience" or "bad conscience." We say, "My conscience is clear," or, "My conscience is bothering me." We talk about freedom of conscience. We refer to a good person as conscientious and to bad conduct as unconscionable. But what is *conscience*?

Basically, conscience is the power of making a judgment between good and evil. The judgment has to do with how moral principles and values apply to a concrete situation. Conscience answers the question: "What is the right thing for me to do here and now?"

An appropriate answer depends upon three elements: knowledge, evaluation, and application.

First, we must know what is right in general. We need to have assimilated from family, neighbors, school, and Church the general demands of goodness, of moral behavior. We have to know what the moral "rules" are, rules which are rooted in teachings about God and humanity, about good and bad.

Second, we need to evaluate the specific circumstances in which we find ourselves. Which circumstances in a situation are important and which are not? Which are of primary importance and which are secondary?

Third, we need to apply the moral principles and values to our specific circumstances. This implies discerning the fit between our circumstances, as we have analyzed them, and the moral principles and values according to which we direct our lives.

Conscience, then, deals with moral principles and values, with specific circumstances and with the linkage between them. It is then the final norm for judging the morality of our action, here in our life, now. Nothing and no one else can take its place. This is what it means to be guided by our conscience.

Following Conscience

Does this mean that I must follow my conscience even if my conscience is mistaken? Yes, but I am not therefore allowed to do anything I want on the plea that I am following my conscience. Nor may I neglect learning what is right in order to have a conscience that is easier to live with. I have an obligation to follow my conscience, but I also have an equal obligation to form my conscience, to do what is necessary for its proper functioning.

Forming Conscience

To accomplish that, we first need instruction. We need to understand where our life comes from, what its purpose is, how we are to reach the goal set for us beyond ourselves and beyond the whims of the moment, what is important and what is illusionary. For this instruction we turn to the word of God and the teachings of the Church.

God's love gives us guidance through the teaching of the Church. The community of the faithful has not only received the word of God, but also has prayed over it, reflected on it and tried to live it through the ages.

The moral teaching of the Church looks on reality not in terms of individual preferences here and now, but in terms of how the love of God is to be expressed in the life of all the faithful. The formation of our consciences, the assimilation of the Church's moral teaching, is one of the most important tasks we face in life. What we do determines what we become, and in order to do what is right, we first have to *know* what is right.

Doing what is wrong is always harmful; doing what is good is beneficial. Goodness corresponds to reality, to the way in which God created us to live.

If I do wrong, I fly in the face of reality, I inflict injury on myself or others. If I am ignorant of right and wrong, I will make wrong moral judgments about what I am called upon to do. I may be subjectively free of fault because I am following my conscience, erroneous though it is, but the harm is done nonetheless. Refusing to form my conscience properly, refusing to assimilate the moral direction God gives me points me toward spiritual harm and possibly even toward spiritual self-destruction.

Acting Prudently

Of equal importance to forming our consciences properly is knowing how to apply our understanding to concrete circumstances here and now. This is the task of the virtue of prudence. Applying the wrong principles in a concrete situation can be as destructive as not having any principles at all. Persons who try to fit principles and circumstances together incorrectly often end up in a simplistic moral legalism or with a bad case of scruples.

For example, is it right for me to take the offer of a new job with a different employer? In order to answer that question I must analyze the implications of the job which has been offered. Am I able to do the work? Is it honest work? How will I be better off than I am now? And what about my present employer? What obligations am I under? What wider contexts should be considered? How will new employment affect my friendships? My religious life? My family? Inherent in all these questions are moral values dealing with honesty, faithfulness, fraternal charity, religion, and probably some others as well. I must try to apply all these principles to the concrete circumstances of the job offer and reach a decision.

Only I can make that decision; but, when I make it, I am responsible for it. If I have done my best possible job of judging, I have made a conscientious decision; I am in good conscience. If I have knowingly rejected or disregarded some moral principles or values, I have made a wrong decision and my conscience will reproach me for the decision as I reflect on it later.

Freedom of Conscience

Where does freedom of conscience fit into all this? *Freedom of conscience* refers to two different things.

First, since my conscience is the final judge of what I must or may do, nobody may make that judgment for me. I must determine how the categories of right and wrong apply to my circumstances here and now. Nobody else may impose his or her judgment on my conscience. Because I am responsible for the judgment, my conscience is and must be "free." This does not mean that I am free to do whatever I want, or to establish and follow any moral principles I wish. I cannot disregard Church teaching if I do not like or understand it, or because it is demanding. But the judgment I finally make comes from within me and, in that sense, is free.

The second meaning of freedom of conscience concerns the relationship of civil society to my religious beliefs. My conscience is "free" because no government has the right to tell me what I must believe or what religion I am to practice. Those decisions, inherently personal, must be made in the context of a person's relationship with God, not in the context of civil law. Used in this sense, freedom of conscience is the equivalent of freedom of religion.

Fundamentally, conscience is the way in which I discover where goodness and growth lie here and now, the way I assimilate and make my own God's love for this individual human creature.

But our conscience is never completely formed. Nor is its exercise ever completely effortless. There is always room for greater moral maturity, always room for more refined moral choices. That's why conscience remains a tough issue.

Questions for Reflection

1. What steps must we take to form our consciences properly?
2. Is it ever appropriate to second-guess someone else's conscientious decisions?
3. What resources are available to us to assist in the proper formation of our consciences?

CHAPTER THREE

Human Life Issues

The value of human life from conception to natural death is an important component of Church teaching, and one that frequently appears in the headlines. It is the first area of focus for the bishops' statement and it covers such controversial topics as abortion, cloning, stem-cell research, euthanasia and assisted suicide, and capital punishment.

Abortion

The most comprehensive—and inspiring—summary of Catholic teaching on abortion is the 1995 papal encyclical *The Gospel of Life (Evangelium Vitae)*. There, the Holy Father speaks specifically and at great length about abortion, beginning first with the natural-law argument against taking human life. He describes the medical and scientific consensus on when human life begins: "From the time that the ovum is fertilized, a life is begun which is neither that of the father nor the mother; it is rather the life of a new human being with his own growth…. [M]odern genetic science offers clear confirmation. It has demonstrated that from the first instant there is established the program of what this living being will be" (60).

Some people are surprised to learn that the obstetrics textbooks used in the leading medical schools in the country today assume that human lives begin at conception! This is not a theological teaching but a medical fact. The more that science studies the unborn, and the more it develops ultrasound imaging of the unborn child, the more confirming evidence emerges of the child's humanity and truly miraculous development.

Many people still believe that the Catholic Church bases its pro-life stance on the religious belief that a human being is ensouled at the moment of conception. But this is wrong. Pope John Paul II's pro-life encyclical *The Gospel of Life* (1995) acknowledges that you can't scientifically verify when a soul enters the human body. (You sure can't see it under a microscope!) The papal letter notes that it is more likely than not that at the "first appearance of a human life" there is a personal presence, a body/soul unity. But even if this is doubted, the pope says, it remains wrong to kill what is certainly human life from the moment of conception, whether or not it is "ensouled." From this scientific consensus about when and how human life begins, it follows that we should all respect human life from the moment of conception. And you might say that a bottom-line minimum for respecting human life is not destroying it!

Hard Cases

Many question why the Church won't make specific exceptions for abortion in cases of rape and incest, or where there are indications of disability. The Church teaches that human beings have value no matter what the circumstances of their conception or physical or mental condition. Admittedly there may be suffering for the mother or the child if the life is brought to term, but such suffering does not extinguish the unborn person's right to life. The more humane and more Christian response to a violated mother or disabled child is more love—not death!

It should also be remembered that no matter how many times abortion is proposed as a solution to a difficult situation, abortion has a way of creating new, long-lasting problems of its own. According to post-abortion women, abortion taints the expected good result.

Some post-abortion women who became pregnant as a result of rape or incest report that the abortion made them feel further violated. Of the other 99 percent of post-abortion women, many report that, instead of feeling free or happy after the abortion, they feel burdened with guilt and loss.

What about the argument that the Church should make exceptions to its teaching when abortion is medically necessary for the mother's health?

First, while the Church opposes all direct abortions, it does not condemn procedures which result, indirectly, in the loss of the unborn child as a "secondary effect." For example, if a mother is suffering an ectopic pregnancy (a baby is developing in her fallopian tube, not the womb), a doctor may remove the fallopian tube as therapeutic treatment to prevent the mother's death. The infant will not survive long after this, but the intention of the procedure and its action is to preserve the mother's life. It is not a direct abortion.

There also occur, very rarely, situations in which, in order to save the mother's life, the child needs to be delivered early. But this can be done safely with a normal, induced delivery, or a caesarean section.

It is also critical to understand that, while the Church teaches that the act of killing an unborn child is intrinsically bad, it does not teach that the mother who seeks an abortion is also intrinsically bad. There is a difference between condemning an act, and judging the guilt of the actor. Only God can judge these women.

To the woman who has had an abortion, the Church says instead: "How can we reconcile you? How can we help you, first, to face honestly what happened, repent, and be reconciled to the child, to yourself, to your family and to God?" Today, most

Catholic dioceses in the United States sponsor programs of healing for post-abortion women.

Stem-cell Research

What are stem cells and why are they so important? Essentially, stem cells are cells that have the potential to become many different kinds of cells. They are the means by which cells in the body can be replenished. In the very early embryo these cells are *totipotent*—that is, they have the potency to become any kind of body cell.

In adult stem cells, the cells are *pluripotent*—they have the capacity to become a variety of cells, but not all. Scientists hope to obtain lines of these embryonic stem cells—large numbers of them grown from a common source—and coax them into becoming specific kinds of cells.

For example, a biologist recently succeeded in having blood cells from bone marrow grow into nerve cells. Other scientists have recently reported success in having embryonic stem cells grow into three different types of blood cells. The goal of this research is to use these stem cells to develop various tissues that can then be used to repair damaged tissues in the body—heart tissue to repair a damaged heart, nerve tissue to repair a damaged spinal column or reverse the effects of Alzheimer's disease. The research is very interesting, complex, and promising.

Which stem cells should be used for research—adult or embryonic? Many have argued that adult stem cells are difficult to obtain, very hard to coax into developing into other tissues and, consequently, their use would involve much more time and money to obtain the desired results. Up until very recently, this was generally true.

But now research has shown that adult stem cells can be isolated and developed. If this research continues to be successful, there may no reason whatsoever to use embryonic stem cells, which requires destruction of early embryos and poses a serious ethical problem. Many argue that adult stem cells are where the resources for stem-cell research should be directed. Continued success in this area would essentially eliminate the need for embryonic stem cells—and put an end to a major ethical problem.

But the problem is that many scientists and many in Congress prefer to use federal funds to support research on stem cells extracted from *already destroyed* human embryos. Is this ethical?

Over the last few decades there has been a strong affirmation by the pope and bishops that the human embryo is to be valued and, in effect, treated as a person from the time of fertilization forward. It is not to be destroyed or seen as disposable tissue that can be used in research as any other tissue might be. Nor should such embryos be generated specifically for research purposes. This of course is possible, given the technology of in vitro, "outside the body," fertilization. And in fact, one fertility clinic in Virginia has reported that in fact that is exactly what it is doing.

What is the moral status of the early embryo? Pope John Paul II gave his perspective on this debate in an address to President George W. Bush on July 23, 2001, during his papal visit. The pope rearticulated his position on the use of embryos by saying:

> Experience is already showing how a tragic coarsening of consciences accompanies the assault on innocent human life in the womb, leading to accommodation and acquiescence in the face of other related evils such as euthanasia, infanticide and, most recently, proposals for the creation for research purposes of human embryos, destined to be destroyed in the process.

The pope also called for the United States to show the world that we can be masters of—and not products of—technology.

It is important to remember the Church does not wish merely to be a naysayer against development and scientific progress. In fact, the Church is very positive and supportive about advances in science that improve the quality of human life. Most of the world knows that the Church works in many places, often in areas of high poverty, seeking to help liberate the human family from disease. In evaluating how to move ahead, whether it is in the laboratory or in society at large, always we are to remember an underlying principle: to value the dignity of human life.

Cloning

The U.S. bishops have also addressed the matter of human cloning. Their Secretariat for Pro-Life Activities explains that cloning is

> a depersonalized way to reproduce, in which human beings are manufactured in the laboratory to preset specifications. It is not a worthy way to bring a new human being into the world. When done for stem cell research, it involves the moral wrong of all embryonic stem cell research (destroying an innocent human life for possible benefit to others) plus an additional wrong: It creates human beings solely in order to kill them for their cells. This is the ultimate reduction of a fellow human being to a mere means, to an instrument of other people's wishes.

> Serious moral concerns about these practices have been raised by an array of both religious and secular groups, including some who disagree with the Catholic Church about abortion…. The human cloning ban supported by the Church has been approved by the House of Representatives by an overwhelming bipartisan majority. Many other countries (including Canada, France, Australia, Germany and Norway) have passed similar bans. Opposition to the idea of treating early human life as a mere object or commodity in the laboratory transcends religious and political division.

Euthanasia and Assisted Suicide

There are in this country and around the world several organizations dedicated to the promotion and/or legalization of assisted suicide or so-called mercy killing. Forms of assisted suicide, with some formal barriers, are legal in three states: Oregon, Washington, and Montana. Most Reverend Wilton D. Gregory, Archbishop of Atlanta, addressed the issue, reaffirming the Catholic Church's opposition on the grounds that human life is a gift from God and we are simply stewards of that gift. The commandment "Thou shalt not kill" applies to this matter. In addition, human life has been redeemed by Christ, and we are responsible to him. Assisted suicide induces death before its time.

Archbishop Gregory responded to the objection that Church teaching entraps a person in the dying process and promotes more pain and suffering. He said, "Our opposition to physician-assisted suicide is not to hinder freedom but to protect the right to die with human and Christian dignity." Between the two extremes of active euthanasia or assisted suicide and the use of every possible means to prolong life at all costs, the Church offers a third alternative of action that can help to guide the public discussion.

The Church recognizes a person's right to refuse disproportionate medical treatment. What we must safeguard in our society is that a person's informed treatment decisions are respected. The Church also recognizes the need for the proper management of pain. In this regard, we must ensure in the clinical setting that a person need not seek death in order to escape pain.

Finally, the Church recognizes the importance of the interpersonal aspects of human suffering and death. As members of the Church, we offer to the sick and dying our service of charity as a resplendent sign that "God has visited his people" (Luke 7:16).

As good stewards, we believe that death is not the final word, that life is not an absolute good. Therefore, we do not have to keep someone alive "at all costs." The Catholic tradition helps with the details, providing this guidance: ordinary means must be used; extraordinary means are optional.

Ordinary means are medicines or treatments that offer reasonable hope of benefit and can be used without excessive expense, pain, or other inconvenience. Extraordinary means do not offer reasonable hope of benefit or include excessive expense, pain, or other inconvenience. What is important to remember is that "ordinary" and "extraordinary" refer not to the technology but to the treatment in relation to the condition of the patient, that is, to the proportion of benefit and burden the treatment provides the patient (see *Declaration on Euthanasia*, 4).

Many people remember when Cardinal Joseph Bernardin of Chicago decided to stop the treatment for his cancer. The treatment had become extraordinary. He did not kill himself by this choice but did stop efforts that prolonged his dying. He allowed death to occur. This distinction between allowing to die and killing, as in euthanasia or assisted suicide, is of great significance in the Catholic tradition. The rejection of this distinction by several U.S. courts raises serious concerns.

Capital Punishment

Along with the leadership assemblies of many Churches (for example, American Baptists, Disciples of Christ, Episcopalians, Lutherans, and Presbyterians), the U.S. bishops expressed their opposition to the death penalty in a 1980 statement, *Capital Punishment.*

The bishops begin by noting that punishment, "since it involves the deliberate infliction of evil on another," must be justifiable. They acknowledge that the Christian tradition has for a long time recognized a government's right to protect its citizens by using the death penalty in some serious situations. The bishops ask, however, if capital punishment is still justifiable in the present circumstances in the United States.

In this context, the bishops enter the debate about deterrence and retribution. They acknowledge that capital punishment certainly prevents the criminal from committing more crimes, yet question whether it prevents others from doing so. Similarly, concerning retribution, the bishops support the arguments against death as an appropriate form of punishment. The bishops add that reform is a third reason given to justify punishment, but it clearly does not apply in the case of capital punishment. And so they affirm: "We believe that in the conditions of contemporary American society, the legitimate purposes of punishment do not justify the imposition of the death penalty."

As with the debate in our wider society, it is important to move behind the discussion of deterrence and retribution to get to the heart of the bishops' position. The statement does just that, by discussing four related values that would be promoted by the abolition of the death penalty.

First, "abolition (of the death penalty) sends a message that we can break the cycle of violence, that we need not take life for life, that we can envisage more humane and more hopeful and effective responses to the growth of violent crime." The bishops recognize that crime is rooted in the complex reality of contemporary society, including those "social conditions of poverty and injustice which often provide the breeding grounds for serious crime." More attention should go to correcting the root causes of crime than to enlarging death row.

Second, "abolition of capital punishment is also a manifestation of our belief in the unique worth and dignity of each person from the moment of conception, a creature made in the image and likeness of God." This belief, rooted in Scripture and consistently expressed in the social teachings of the Church, applies to all people, including those who have taken life.

Third, "abolition of the death penalty is further testimony to our conviction, a conviction which we share with the Judaic and

Islamic traditions, that God is indeed the Lord of life." And so human life in all its stages is sacred, and human beings are called to care for life, that is, to exercise good stewardship and not absolute control. The bishops recognize that abortion, euthanasia, and the death penalty are not the same issue, but they each point to the same fundamental value: safeguarding the sanctity of life.

Fourth, "we believe that abolition of the death penalty is most consonant with the example of Jesus." In many ways this final point summarizes the other three: the God revealed in the life of Jesus is a God of forgiveness and redemption, of love and compassion—in a word, a God of life. The heart of the bishops' position on the death penalty, then, is found in the gospel.

Gut-level reactions may cry out for vengeance, but Jesus' example in the Gospels invites all to develop a new and different attitude toward violence. The bishops encourage us to embody Jesus' message in practical and civic decisions.

Clearly, the Hebrew Scriptures allowed the death penalty. Yet, as we see in Ezekiel and many other passages, there is also an attempt to limit violence and to stress mercy. In the Christian Scriptures, Jesus' life and teachings (see the Sermon on the Mount, Matthew 5:1—7:29) focus on mercy, reconciliation, and redemption. The basic thrust of the Gospels supports opposition to the death penalty.

Indeed, the early Church (for example, in the writings of Clement of Rome and Justin Martyr) generally found taking human life to be incompatible with the gospel. Christians were not to participate in capital punishment. Later, after Christianity became the religion of the Roman Empire, opposition to the death penalty declined. Augustine recognized the death penalty as a means of deterring the wicked and protecting the innocent. In the Middle Ages, Thomas Aquinas reaffirmed this position.

The *Catechism of the Catholic Church* reflects this tradition, stating that the death penalty is possible in cases of extreme gravity. However, the *Catechism* adds:

> If bloodless means [that is, other than killing] are suffi-cient to defend human lives against an aggressor and to protect public order and the safety of persons, public authority should limit itself to such means, because they better correspond to the concrete conditions of the common good and are more in conformity to the dignity of the human person. (*CCC*, #2267)

Clearly, then, the bishops' opposition to the death penalty is in accord with universal Church teaching.

Homosexuality and Same-sex Marriage

Richard Sparks, C.S.P., has explained the Church's view on homo-sexuality, drawing on the USCCB's document *Human Sexuality.* He notes:

> The Catholic Church has embraced the core moral dis-

tinction between being homosexual in orientation and the choice of doing (or not doing) homosexual sexual acts. The Catholic bishops in the United States noted in their 1990 document *Human Sexuality* that "The distinction between being homosexual, and doing homosexual genital actions, while not always clear and convincing, is a helpful and important one when dealing with the complex issue of homosexuality, particularly in the educational and pastoral arena" (56).

As the Catholic bishops state it, "[W]e believe that it is only within a heterosexual marital relationship that genital sexual activity is morally acceptable. Only within marriage does sexual intercourse fully symbolize the Creator's dual design, as an act of covenant love, with the potential of co-creating new human life. Therefore, homosexual genital activity is considered immoral" (*Human Sexuality,* 55). In somewhat less pastoral, more philosophical terms, Vatican documents use the phrase "intrinsically disordered" when referring to homosexual genital acts.

Whatever the term chosen, the implication would be the same: that sexual intercourse is designed by God both (1) as an act of lovemaking, of two-in-one-flesh union, and also (2) as the means to procreate new life, to co-create—as a couple and with God's grace—new members of the human species. If these are the indelible meanings of sexual intimacy, written, as it were, into human nature and the nature of these intimate acts, then homosexual sex seems to be essentially deficient or incomplete.

The U.S. bishops have clarified the Church's opposition to same-sex marriages. In November of 2003 the bishops' document *Between Man and Woman* repeated the Church's conviction that marriage, as instituted by God, is a faithful, exclusive, lifelong union of a man and a woman joined in an intimate community of life and love. They commit themselves completely to each other and to the wondrous responsibility of bringing children into the world and caring for them.

Between Man and Woman states, in part:

> The natural structure of human sexuality makes man and woman complementary partners for the transmission of human life. Only a union of male and female can express the sexual complementarity willed by God for marriage. The permanent and exclusive commitment of marriage is the necessary context for the expression of sexual love intended by God both to serve the transmission of human life and to build up the bond between husband and wife (see *CCC*, #1639–1640).
>
> . . .

For several reasons a same-sex union contradicts the nature of marriage: It is not based on the natural complementarity of male and female; it cannot cooperate with God to create new life; and the natural purpose of sexual union cannot be achieved by a same-sex union. Persons in same-sex unions cannot enter into a true conjugal union. Therefore, it is wrong to equate their relationship to a marriage.

Marriage is a basic human and social institution. Though it is regulated by civil laws and Church laws, it did not originate from either the Church or state, but from God. Therefore, neither church nor state can alter the basic meaning and structure of marriage.

The issue of same-sex marriage is particularly sensitive for the Church because one of its duties and privileges is presiding at the sacrament of matrimony. The Church must stand firm on its view of marriage in defense of all those who have chosen this vocation. At the same time, the Church does not condemn people who are attracted to members of the same sex and does not want to alienate those who already suffer far too much condemnation and alienation. Where the Church's view on homosexuality might seem discriminatory, it can sometimes be helpful to remember that the Church cautions against all extramarital sex, whether homosexual or heterosexual. This is not to suggest that sexual expression is in any way "shameful," but rather to underscore its value in a lifelong, loving relationship.

Questions for Reflection

1. How do the Church's views on these issues form support for a consistent ethic of life—a belief in the value of all human life?

2. Do you understand the Church's views on such complicated issues as stem-cell research, cloning, and assisted suicide? How do these apply to everyday life?

3. Is the death penalty justifiable when there are alternative means of protecting the public from dangerous criminals?

CHAPTER FOUR

Responsibility for the World

When Pope Paul VI, on October 4, 1965, stood before the General Assembly of the United Nations and pleaded, "No more war, war never again," the Church for a moment took center stage in world events and offered its moral teaching as a guide for peace on earth. The Church's eyes are focused on the kingdom of heaven but its feet are firmly planted on *terra firma*. The questions Jesus posed at his second coming make it clear that the Church cannot ignore the world around us: "When I was hungry, thirsty, naked, sick, in prison, did you respond?" (see Matthew 25:35). Social justice is integral to life, liberty and the pursuit of happiness. It is also the agenda of the Church.

Catholics and all people of good will instinctively know that they must work to avoid war and promote peace. Nations have an obligation to defend themselves against terrorism and other forms of aggression, but the means to the end must be proportionate. The complexities of international relations and the ideologies which seek world domination make prospects for peace tenuous and planning for security unavoidable. But all decisions must take into account the dignity of human beings and the sacredness of human life.

Social Justice

All human beings have a right to a particular reverence and respect simply because they are creatures of a loving God. Just as the individual person must respect the dignity of all other human beings, so also an economic system must respect the dignity of all human beings. Any arrangement which enslaves human beings, causes them to live without hope, or uses them as disposable means for purposes beyond themselves is an immoral arrangement because it is in disaccord with the demands of human dignity.

Equally fundamental is the principle of the human community. Nobody lives all alone in the world and nobody can survive without interacting with others. Each of us must receive from others, and each of us must give to others. We depend on each other for food, clothing, protection and for many other things as well. Not one of us can be excluded from the human community; we all have the right and the responsibility to participate.

On the basis of these principles, the Church teaches that every approach to social and political life that claims to be humane, moral, and Christian must be shaped by three questions: What does the system do *for* people? What does it do *to* people? And how do people *participate*? The basic issue implicit in these questions is how human dignity is protected and promoted.

The ramifications of all this are far-reaching. These basic moral principles provide the yardstick to measure the morality of the way a society distributes wealth, the criteria it uses in the exercise of power, its attitudes toward the poor, the protection it provides to individuals and to families and a thousand other matters. The application of the principles is not always easy, and even people who agree about the principles can sometimes disagree about their application. But the principles are there, and they are moral principles.

Obviously we do not bear personal responsibility for the origin of the injustices and inequities in our present economic system. Nor do we bear the responsibility to change the system single-handedly. But we are responsible for dealing with injustice to the extent to which we are able. We are responsible for making an individual contribution to efforts and attitudes aimed at protecting and promoting human dignity.

This means being aware of the realities. We can easily close our eyes to the needs of those around us—and still more easily overlook the needs of those far away.

It also means trying to use individual resources wisely and justly and common resources fairly. Is my salary all for me, or do I see that others have a claim on it too? What kind of a consumer am I? Do I buy, use up, and throw away everything which media advertising says I am supposed to buy, use up, and throw away?

Our personal convictions constitute a major element in our relationship with the society around me. Do we accept the prejudices of the system: "People are poor because they don't want to work," "I am prosperous only because of my own efforts," "Only the wealthy have the right to power"? Or do we test so-called common wisdom with Christian standards? What issues do we take into account when we vote? Do we even vote?

Some believers have the talents and opportunities to engage in economic or political activity on a wider, more public scale. Catholic teaching invites them to see these possibilities as a call to serve humanity in a special way. Being in business or politics offers an opportunity to work for the dignity of humankind in a way that few others enjoy.

Social justice is a tough issue partly because it is so big. Even if we are clear about why the Church teaches about these matters, the scope and implications of the teaching are so vast that they are difficult to grasp. Moreover, we are tempted to see our individual efforts as insignificant. But the fact remains that our loving God is concerned about the economic and social structures in which we live, just as God is concerned about the actions and attitudes of all the individuals who determine, however remotely, what those structures are to be.

The Just War Theory

At their conference in 1983, the U.S. bishops assessed the morality of war in the twentieth century, particularly in the light of nuclear weapons. Their pastoral letter, *The Challenge of Peace: God's Promise and Our Response*, was the result of three years of intense work that included a wide process of consultation of experts, three drafts that were widely circulated and commented upon, and a comprehensive review of the best theological and military literature of the day.

The Church developed its teaching on the Just War as war victimized more and more people. World War II, while considered a just war on the whole by most people, was also a transition war. It carried many horrors, including the millions of victims of the Holocaust, the millions of civilians killed, the high number of military casualties, the development and use of nuclear weapons, and the arms race that immediately followed. How did the just war theory fare in the light of these events?

Pope Pius XII made a variety of comments about war during his pontificate (1939–1958), but it was the American theologian John Courtney Murray, s.j., who brought together these various strands of teaching into a coherent whole. His summary, presented in his 1960 book *We Hold These Truths*, is an important starting point and is also a critical point of reference for the discussions that led to *The Challenge of Peace*.

The first point of his summary is that all wars of aggression are prohibited. Violence unleashed by war is a disproportionate means to achieve justice. If individual states continue to engage in aggressive wars, international structures will be much more difficult to develop.

The second point is that a defensive war to redress injustice is possible only if four conditions are fulfilled: (1) the nation must have been attacked; (2) war is the last resort; (3) there is a proportion between the harm suffered and the violence released by war; and (4) there are limits to the use of force, namely, civilians are off-limits and no weapons (such as the proposed neutron bomb) that would destroy all human life within their range are permissible.

The third summary point is that preparations for a country's self-defense are legitimate because the right of self-defense cannot be denied to any nation and there is no international body that controls arms. Finally, Murray holds in common with Pius XII a position that later theologians rejected: that once war has been justly declared by the proper authority of a country, no Catholic can be a conscientious objector.

Murray's *We Hold These Truths* is an important summary of the just war teaching from World War II through the 1980s. It served as a guide for discussions of the wars in Korea and

Vietnam as well as other conflicts involving the United States. Yet changing times and events—a growing number of nuclear weapons, the military and moral complexities of deterrence theory, and the growing realization of the global consequences of nuclear war—began to force new questions. The need for a reevaluation of just war theory became apparent.

In *The Challenge of Peace: God's Promise and Our Response,* the bishops examine the signs of the times, consider the gospel mandate, evaluate and test the application of moral principles, and consider the implications of these reflections. They develop a perspective that suggests certain conclusions and actions that they think are coherent with a rightly formed Christian conscience.

The bishops recognize the complexity of the issue before them and recognize that a rigorous consideration of the moral issues regarding nuclear war does not lead to one obvious moral conclusion or completely rule out different points of view. They propose a framework for thinking through the problem and recognize that on some issues there will be a plurality of solutions.

They recognize, of course, that there are universally binding moral principles such as civilian immunity, but also that there will be prudential judgments that are based on specific circumstances. Thus the bishops acknowledge that even though all might hold the same principles, there will be a diversity of moral judgments reached about nuclear war.

The document restates long-held Catholic teaching on war and its moral conduct. First is the traditional *jus ad bellum*, the criteria for justly declaring war. These are just cause, competent authority, comparative justice, right intention, last resort, and probability of success. A final reason is proportionality, assessing a relation between the violence of war and the good to be achieved. These criteria seek to ensure that the proper authority assesses the situation and seeks other remedies before declaring that the situation demands the use of force.

The second set of criteria has to do with what is called *jus in bello*, moral norms for conducting war. The two traditional criteria here are proportionality and discrimination. Proportionality in this sense says that the response to aggression must not exceed the nature of the aggression. The criterion of discrimination prohibits direct attacks on civilians or noncombatants and seeks to limit as much as possible any harm even if unintended. War's damage must be limited, particularly its harms to civilians.

The bishops' document, *The Challenge of Peace*, is remarkable for a number of reasons. First, it is clear in its support of pacifism and conscientious objection as legitimate positions for a Catholic. This was important because Pius XII argued that once war was legitimately declared by the state, no Catholic could be a conscientious objector. His position, passed over by Vatican II, was strongly rejected by this letter. The *Catechism of the Catholic Church* presents this newer development but also argues that such objectors must serve the community in some other way.

Second, there is a major shift in the U.S. bishops' letter, a shift not fully articulated in the *Catechism*. The traditional assumption was that force was acceptable when used to redress a violation of justice. This goes back to St. Augustine, who taught that war is justified as an act of love to remedy an injustice that has been done to one's own country or to a neighbor's country. Love may resort to force to restrain an enemy who harms another, the U.S. bishops teach. But the bishops also assert that peace is preferable to war. One has to have serious reasons to override this presumption in favor of peace, a rejection of the traditional position of Augustine that violence is an appropriate means of vindicating injustice.

Third, the document affirms that each state must recognize that it does not have absolute justice on its side. The purpose of this criterion is to temper one's claims to a just cause and thus also exert a restraint on the use of force.

The U.S. bishops have relied on *The Challenge of Peace* in drawing up two statements about the war in Iraq. In their statement of November of 2002, the bishops express their grave concerns over the expansion of just cause to include preventive wars. In terms of legitimate authority, the bishops request that both the U.S. government and the United Nations be involved in the decision making.

The U.S. bishops, with strong support from Pope John Paul II, express serious concern about the problem of unpredictable consequences in Iraq and in the rest of the Middle East. They are deeply concerned about wider conflict and unrest in that area of the world. They raise significant moral concern about the cost and burdens to be borne by the civilian population of Iraq. The statement concludes with the request to continue to seek peaceful resolutions.

The bishops spoke again in February 2003, immediately prior to the U.S. invasion, once again with the strong support of the pope. Their statement was highly critical of "preemptive, unilateral use of military force... [because this] would create deeply troubling moral and legal precedents." Then the bishops made this remarkable statement: "Based on the facts that are known, it is difficult to justify resort to war against Iraq, lacking clear and adequate evidence of an imminent attack of a grave nature or Iraq's involvement in the terrorist attacks of September 11."

Church leaders did not change their position during the course of the war, nor have the events of the invasion and withdrawal of U.S. troops from Iraq in 2011 invalidated their position.

Migration/Immigration

In 2003 the Catholic Bishops of the United States and of Mexico issued a joint letter on migration, *Strangers No Longer: Together on the Journey of Hope.* They pointed to an ever-growing interdependence and integration of Mexicans and Americans. Hundreds of thousands of Mexicans enter the United States every day; a significant number of U.S. citizens live, work, and retire in Mexico. These migration/immigration statistics verify a world-wide phenomenon often called globalization. The bishops agreed that migration between the two nations is necessary and beneficial, but they also recognized the multiple challenges which accompany it.

The bishops stated that the Church's social teaching provides a

> basis for the development of basic principles regarding the right to migrate for those attempting to exercise their God-given human rights. Catholic teaching also states that the root causes of migration—poverty, injustice, religious intolerance, armed conflicts—must be addressed so that migrants can remain in their homeland and support their families.

Referring to papal teaching on the matter, they further noted that:

> In his landmark encyclical *Pacem in Terris,* Blessed Pope John XXIII expands the right to migrate as well as the right to not have to migrate: "Every human being has the right to freedom of movement and of residence within the confines of his own country; and, when there are just reasons for it, the right to emigrate to

other countries and take up residence there" (25). Pope John XXIII placed limits on immigration, however, when there are "just reasons for it." Nevertheless, he stressed the obligation of sovereign states to promote the universal good where possible, including an obligation to accommodate migration flows. For more powerful nations, a stronger obligation exists.

The bishops noted that both episcopal conferences confirmed the long tradition of Church teachings on issues relating to migration. They outlined five principles characteristic of these teachings:

1. Persons have the right to find opportunities in their homeland
2. Persons have the right to migrate to support themselves and their families
3. Sovereign nations have the right to control their borders
4. Refugees and asylum seekers should be afforded protection
5. The human dignity and human rights of undocumented migrants should be respected

The bishops' statement called on the governments of both countries to cooperate and to jointly enact policies that will create a generous, legal flow of migrants between both nations, stating:

Of particular concern are the border enforcement policies pursued by both governments that have contributed to the abuse and even deaths of migrants in both Mexico and the United States.

Along the United States-Mexico border, the U.S. government has launched several border-blockade initiatives in the past decade designed to discourage undocumented migrants from entering the country. Rather than significantly reducing illegal crossings, the initiatives have instead driven migrants into remote and dangerous areas of the southwest region of the United States, leading to an alarming number of migrant deaths.

The letter urges both the U.S. and Mexican enforcement authorities to "abandon the type of strategies that give rise to migrant smuggling operations and migrant deaths." Only a long-term effort that adjusts economic inequalities between the United States and Mexico will provide Mexican workers with employment opportunities that will allow them to remain at home and to support themselves and their families. The creation of employment opportunities in Mexico would help to reduce poverty and would mitigate the incentive for many to look for employment in the United States.

Economic Challenges

There is no Catholic teaching that will provide all the answers for economic stability. Nevertheless Fr. Richard M. Gula, S.S., suggests that certain virtues or natural capacities need to be cultivated during tough economic times. He recalls a truism of moral theology, namely, who we are affects what we do, and what we do affects who we become.

Fr. Gula's analysis proposes that virtue links us to right action by leaning us toward what human well-being demands. "The current economic crisis" he says, "causes us to ask, 'What kind of persons shall we *be* to face these trying times?'" He suggests five specific virtues or strengths of character will help, namely, gratitude, generosity, solidarity, courage, and hope.

Gratitude opens the imagination to an economy not based on Wall Street—the economy of grace. It is our window into the deepest reality shaping our lives: God's love for us. The affirmation on which gratitude depends—that God is good and wills our well-being—doesn't always seem to be true. A lost job, a foreclosed home, and a devastated retirement fund are cases in point. But misfortunes can cause us to re-examine the meaning of life. It can cause us to pause and consider the value of all undeserved benefits we have received.

Generosity flows from gratitude. It means giving over rather than giving up. In a time of financial crisis being generous is countercultural where self-interest trumps service. It is the virtue of the good neighbor. We cannot imitate Christ without being in relationship with others and sharing our gifts with those in need.

Preferential Option for the Poor

On March 26, 1991, Bishop Kenneth E. Untener of Saginaw, Michigan, issued a "decree" that from that day forward, until July 1, 1991, all meetings held under Church auspices, at the parish or diocesan level, no matter what their purpose, must begin with the agenda item: How shall what we are doing here affect or involve the poor?

Bishop Untener was simply trying to get the people of his diocese, especially diocesan and parochial leaders, to recognize the human (and Christian) obligation to be concerned for the needy members of society. His experiment brought to light several insights that are pertinent to how we Americans ought to vote.

He noted that the poor are usually invisible, that is, they are not present for church services or committees, do not frequent shopping malls or supermarkets, cannot afford parochial school tuition. He said, "It takes initiative and creativity to reach the poor."

"The undeserving poor," he soon found, were easily dismissed even by good people. People tended to respond to those in abject poverty, but if there was a hint that the poor man was poor through his own fault, the old bromide about "helping oneself" often came to the fore. The bishop suggested that we be less judgmental, and if we are to err, let us err on the side of largesse. He also discovered that helping the poor is not always a pleasant experience, that sometimes in helping the poor you'll get taken, but he also discovered that many times it is the poor who help the poor.

When the ninety-seven days of his decree ended, Bishop Untener asked himself, "Is it all over? Can we now get back to normal?" Yes, he decided. We can get back to normal by realizing that "normal" means talking about the poor at normal meetings, and finding ways to translate our words into actions. "Normal" means focusing on the poor as much as Jesus did.

In his estimation the decree was successful, but it was like the success of someone who joined Weight Watchers and reached his or her goal by losing thirty-seven pounds. The "loser" is congratulated, cheered by all at the meeting and given a pin. But the true measure of success is whether the loser will change his eating habits in the weeks and months and years ahead. Some do, and some don't.

Sometimes elected officials have no knowledge of or concern for the poor. Community councils may enact legislation to keep the poor away. Decisions about public housing may be made without regard to the needs of all citizens in the area. NIMBY— "not in my back yard"—is a frequent cry. The Church's concern for the poor (prompted by the example Jesus gave) ought to inform a Catholic voter's choices for public officials, levies, and legislation.

Health Care

The Church is concerned about health-care reform in this country today because the Church has been part of health care in this country from the beginning. In fact, the Church's involvement in health-care systems long predates the United States, going back to the Middle Ages. During those years, various religious groups—religious and lay, composed of women or men—cared for the needs of the sick and often lived among the sick poor.

As Catholic health-care systems worked more closely with other health-care institutions over the years, a need arose for some guidelines on how our faith informs practice in a Catholic facility. This need became especially pressing in modern times, as U.S. health care began taking on increasingly complex ethical issues. The U.S. Catholic bishops created such guidelines, the *Ethical and Religious Directives for Catholic Health Care Services* published to help guide Catholic hospitals and other Catholic health-care facilities as they serve in the name of the Church.

The guidelines begin with a section devoted to the social responsibility of Catholic health-care institutions, laying out five values regarding the social responsibility of Catholic health-care institutions.

First and foremost, "Catholic health-care ministry is rooted in a commitment to promote and defend human dignity; this is the foundation of its concern to respect the sacredness of every human life from the moment of conception until death." Second comes the promotion of the common good. From these two pivotal values, the guidelines derive three other principles of our social justice tradition and apply them to health care: care for the poor, responsible stewardship and the rights of conscience.

This attention to the Catholic social tradition, however, has not been without conflict. The needs of the community are likely always to be greater than the capacity of Catholic health care to satisfy those needs. In some situations hospitals find that the values from the Church's directives are in conflict with one another. The call to be responsible stewards, for example, limits the amount of charity care a hospital can give. The hospital must, along with ensuring care for the poor and vulnerable, pay its employees a just wage.

Ecological Concerns

In *Care for Creation: A Franciscan Spirituality of the Earth,* Ilia Delio, O.S.F., Keith Douglass Warner, O.F.M., and Pamela Wood, express the spiritual side of ecological concerns. They believe that human beings are the cause of our planet's environmental crises. We have, they say, no one else to blame. We are all responsible to some degree in these unfolding tragedies, and we are all bearing some of the negative effects. The biodiversity crisis and global climate change threaten the integrity of God's creation, but pollution of all kinds threatens the bodily integrity and medical health of everyone.

The authors' analysis addresses what they call "the grim news," namely that because of Americans' high-consumption lifestyle, the average American has an annual ecological "footprint" of twenty-four acres, the greatest per-person impact in the world (see www.myfootprint.org for more information). It would take five Earths full of resources to supply the entire human family with an American lifestyle. For reference, the global average is about seven acres per person, but even that level of consumption cannot be maintained indefinitely. It takes about fifteen months of biological productivity to support the annual global average of consumption. Simply put, we humans are living beyond our ecological means.

We Americans share the planet with more than seven billion humans. Reducing our consumption is simultaneously an ecological and social justice issue. Reducing our consumption levels is the most important environmental task before us. It means that each of us has a duty to learn more about our impact on the world around us and to make prudent changes to reduce the damage we do to the environment. More challenging is learning how we can change the economic and political structures that are most destructive to the long-term health of the planet, without destroying the livelihood of those dependent upon the current structures.

Questions for Reflection

1. What do you think are the most important facets of the Church's teaching on social justice?

2. Why are the poor more worthy of our consideration than the wealthy?

3. How can you become more mindful of your impact on global trade or ecology with each small action or purchase?

Sources

Alvaré, Helen. "Abortion: What the Church Teaches." *Catholic Update*, August 1998.

Delio, Ilia O.S.F., Keith Douglass Warner, O.F.M., and Pamela Wood. *Care for Creation: A Franciscan Spirituality of the Earth* (Cincinnati: St. Anthony Messenger Press, 2008).

Gregory, Wilton D., S.L.D. "Why the Church Opposes Assisted Suicide." *Catholic Update*, August 1997.

Gula, Richard M., S.S. "Five Virtues for Hard Economic Times." *Catholic Update,* August 2009.

Nairn, Fr. Thomas, O.F.M. "Catholics and Health Care: They Go Together." *Catholic Update*, July 2010.

Overberg, Kenneth R., S.J. "A Consistent Ethic of Life." *Catholic Update,* July 1998.

———. "The Death Penalty: Why the Church Speaks a Countercultural Message." *Catholic Update*, January 1995.

———. "End of Life Ethics: Preparing for the Hour of Death." *Catholic Update*, August 2006.

Pilarczyk, Archbishop Daniel E. *Twelve Tough Issues—and More: What the Church Teaches and Why* (Cincinnati: St. Anthony Messenger Press, 2002).

Shannon, Thomas A. "What Is 'Just War' Today?" *Catholic Update,* May 2004.

———. "Stem-cell Research: How Catholic Ethics Guide Us." *Catholic Update*, January 2002.

Sparks, Richard, C.S.P. "What the Church Teaches About Homosexuality." *Catholic Update,* July 1999.

Untener, Bishop Kenneth E. "How Should We Think About the Poor? A Bishop Reflects." *Catholic Update*, July 1992.

USCCB. "Faithful Citizenship: The Challenge of Forming Consciences." *Catholic Update*, June 2008.

———."Stem Cell Research and Human Cloning: Questions and Answers." *Catholic Update*, January 2007.

———. "Between Man and Woman: Questions and Answers About Marriage and Same-Sex Unions." *Catholic Update*, March 2004.

——— and Conferencia del Episcopado Mexicano. *Strangers No Longer: Together on the Journey of Hope* (Washington, D.C.: USCCB, 2002).

Contributors

Helen Alvaré served as director of planning and information for the U.S. Catholic bishops' secretariat for pro-life activities and is a freelance writer. She teaches law at George Mason University in Arlington, Virginia.

John Feister is editor-in-chief of periodicals at Franciscan Media. He holds master's degrees in humanities and in theology from Xavier University, Cincinnati.

Wilton D. Gregory, S.L.D., has been the archbishop of Atlanta since 2005. He was president of the USCCB from 2001 to 2004.

Richard M. Gula, a Sulpician priest, is a professor of moral theology at the Franciscan School of Theology/Graduate Theological Union, Berkeley, California. His books include *The Good Life* and *The Call to Holiness* (Paulist).

Norman Langenbrunner has served as a high school teacher, associate pastor, and parish pastor. He has written articles for *Liguorian*, *The Bible Today*, *St Anthony Messenger*, and *Catechist*.

Thomas Nairn, O.F.M., is the senior director of ethics at the Catholic Health Association, U.S.A. He holds a Ph.D. from the University of Chicago Divinity School and has given lectures and workshops around the world.

Kenneth R. Overberg, s.j., a Jesuit priest, has a Ph.D. in Christian ethics from the University of Southern California. He is a professor of theology at Xavier University, Cincinnati, and is a regular *Catholic Update* contributor. He is the author of *Conscience in Conflict: How to Make Moral Choices* and *Into the Abyss of Suffering* (St. Anthony Messenger Press).

Daniel E. Pilarczyk served as archbishop of Cincinnati from 1982 to 2009. He was president of the National Conference of Catholic Bishops 1989 to 1992. His books include *Being Catholic: How We Believe, Practice and Think* and *Live Letters: Reflections on the Second Readings of the Sunday Lectionary* (St. Anthony Messenger Press).

Thomas A. Shannon is a professor of religion and social ethics in the department of humanities and arts at Worcester Polytechnic Institute, Worcester, Massachusetts. He is the author of several books and many articles on bioethics.

Richard Sparks, c.s.p., holds a Ph.D. in ethics from the Catholic University of America. He is a popular lecturer on ethics, serves as ethical consultant to hospitals, and is associate pastor at Old St. Mary's Church in Chicago.

Bishop Kenneth E. Untener, a native of Detroit, was ordained to the priesthood by Cardinal John Dearden in 1963. After parish and chancery work, he obtained a doctorate in theology from the Gregorian University in Rome and then returned to Detroit. He served as bishop of the Diocese of Saginaw from 1980 to his death in 2004.